From Start to Finis

MY LIFE AS A CHRISTIAN

- Trevor Guy
- Sue Mizon
- Paul Morgan

DREF WEN

The Lord's Prayer

Our Father who art in heaven,
Hallowed be thy name.
Thy kingdom come,
Thy will be done
On earth as it is in heaven.
Give us this day our daily bread,
And forgive us our trespasses
As we forgive them that trespass against us.
And lead us not into temptation
But deliver us from evil.
For thine is the kingdom, the power and the glory,
For ever and ever,
Amen.

Special Photography Pat and Charles Aithie (ffotograff)

Design Michael Leaman Design Partnership

The books in this series are also available in Welsh-language editions.

Photographs B. O'Donnell (ffotograff) page 12 top; Trevor Guy (ESIS) pages 3 foot left, 10, 11, 16, 19 centre, 20 foot, 21 all, 22 all, 23, 24 foot left and right, 28 top, 29 right, 32 foot, 37 centre, 54 all, 55 top, 57 foot right, 58 all, 60 all; Salvation Army Archives page 13 foot. All other photographs are by Pat and Charles Aithie (ffotograff). Some of these (often indicated by corner mountings) are reproduced from photographs kindly provided by the families concerned. *Map* Pat and Charles Aithie (ffotograff) page 10. We have made every effort to contact owners of copyright material and apologise if in any instance we have been unsuccessful.

First published 1999 by Gwasg y Dref Wen, 28 Church Road, Whitchurch, Cardiff CF14 2EA. Telephone 029 20617860.
Reprinted 2001, 2003.
Printed in Hong Kong.

Contents

Introduction

In this book you will meet several different young people. The one thing they all have in common is that they belong to the Christian religion.

Not all Christians follow their religion in the same way. Christians who have similar beliefs and forms of worship often form their own grouping within Christianity, called a denomination. There are many Christian denominations. To give you a good idea of the variety within Christianity these are the young people who appear in the book and the denominations to which they belong.

IORI I belong to the Church in Wales. Until 1920 our Church used to be part of the Church of England. The two Churches are still very similar.

REBECCA I belong to the Roman Catholic Church. The Pope, who lives in Rome, is our leader.

PHILIPPA I am a member of the Baptist Church. We baptise people when they are old enough to make their own minds up about being a Christian.

SIONED I belong to the Presbyterian Church. Presbyter means "elder". Our church is run by elders who have been chosen by others in the church as the leaders.

DAVINIA My church is the Pentecostal Church. It has a name like the festival of Pentecost because we believe in letting the Spirit of God into our lives. It makes us glad to be alive.

RUTH I am a member of the Salvation Army. We wear a uniform like soldiers but we don't fight for land or to hurt people. We are fighting to do God's work.

My community 1

Iori: *The church is one of the main meeting points in the area. We sometimes prepare plays to perform in the church.*

IORI We moved to Brechfa a few years ago when my father became the **vicar** here. At school I really like science and I spend time reading science fiction stories. I come to church because it's a habit, but also because I choose to. There's a good sense of community to our church, a feeling of togetherness.

REBECCA I go to school near Llanelli. There are four in the family: my mother Sandra, my father Willi, my sister Anna and me. My friends only speak Welsh, so in school we speak a lot of Welsh. My father was brought up in Germany and we have been there on our holidays lots of times. The people aren't different, only the language.

I don't think there are enough things for people my age to do, apart from going to places like youth clubs. I meet my Catholic friends every Sunday in church when we go to **Mass**. But I don't see much of them until the next Sunday because we're rather scattered. Everybody is Catholic in the area of Germany where my father comes from.

Rebecca: *It's important to me that we are part of the Catholic family.*

THINK ABOUT:

What is a community? What do you think Iori means when he talks about "a good sense of community"?

Are the friends you see out of school the same ones as those you have in school? What are the problems and pleasures of having different sets of friends?

Different communities in Britain speak different languages. Why are people keen to keep using the language that their families have always spoken?

Philippa: I've run the 8,000 metres and came joint first.

Philippa: My family is a Christian family.

FACT FILE

Vicar The person who is specially trained to lead the worship and look after the people in the parish, the area which the church serves.

Mass A special service when bread and wine are taken to remember Jesus.

PHILIPPA

My family is quite big. There are eight of us. I have four sisters and one brother. I like netball and long-distance running. I live in Peniel now, but we moved here from England five years ago.

THINGS TO DO

Draw three circles in different colours which overlap:

In the green circle write names of friends.
In the red circle write names of family.
In the blue circle write names of people you know at school.

Where the groups overlap, for example if you have a friend you know from school, write their names in the space where the circles overlap. Can you put anyone right in the middle where all three overlap?

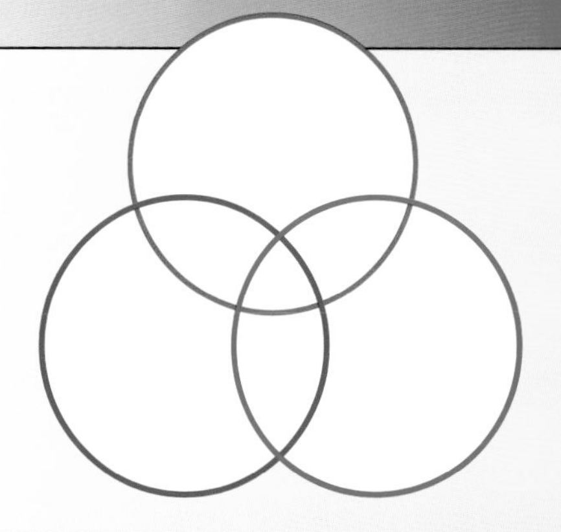

Make a poster for your local community to advertise all the different things there are for people to do. Try to include things for different age groups and for religious groups.

Philippa lives with her mother, father and her five brothers and sisters. What do you think are the advantages and disadvantages of living in a big family? Would you prefer to live in a large or small family? Write a paragraph to say what you think.

My community 2

SIONED I live in Llanfairpwll with Mam and Dad and my brother Gethin. Our village has the longest place name in Britain, but it's Llanfairpwll for short. I like PE best at school and play wing attack in the netball team. I've been going to Sunday School since I was very small.

DAVINIA I live in Caerleon, near Newport, but my family come from Jamaica. We have relatives in America, Leeds, Birmingham, London and other places. We keep in close touch with most of them.

I love school and I've got lots of friends there. In church I have a different group of friends. They come from all around Newport to go to our church. I like going there because you learn different things. You learn to understand each other. We all look after each other, it's like one big family. When someone is ill everyone asks after them and goes to visit them.

Sioned: *I like Sunday School each week. We meet other children and join the adults for part of the service in the chapel.*

THINK ABOUT:

Most of Sioned's friends don't go to Sunday School. Are your interests shared by your friends or do you do things which your friends don't join in?

Why does Davinia go to church? Are her reasons different from Iori's reasons for going to church?

How do Ruth's friends know she is a Christian?

Why do you think Christians get together on a Sunday?

Davinia: *I like music and at church I sing in the choir. Belonging to the church can be fun because you meet more people.*

RUTH I live in Cwm which is near Ebbw Vale. I go to the Welsh school in Pontypool. I have one brother, Richard, who goes to the same school. My mum works in the baker's shop just down the road and my dad's a teacher. We all belong to the Salvation Army **Corps** in Cwm. The hall where we hold our meetings is just round the corner from our house.

I only wear my uniform on Sunday, but my friends at school know I'm a Christian and belong to the Salvation Army because they ask me things like, "What do you do on a Sunday?" They're interested in what I do, probably because none of them go to any sort of church.

FACT FILE

Corps The people who worship and work together in each Salvation Army community. It is called a Corps because they are organised like soldiers, but to serve God. Each Corps has its own set of officers to lead it.

Ruth: *Everyone is very friendly round here. It's a small place.*

THINGS TO DO

In Davinia's church community they help each other in all sorts of ways. Imagine you belong to a group of young people who want to help in their local community. Design an advert which will tell people the ways in which you could help them for free.

Ruth likes living where she does. Write a letter to a pen-friend who has never been to your area and tell your friend what you like or dislike about living there.

Ruth's friends ask her, "What do you do on a Sunday?" Write a diary for yourself for one Sunday, setting out how you spend the day.

How my religion began: Jesus

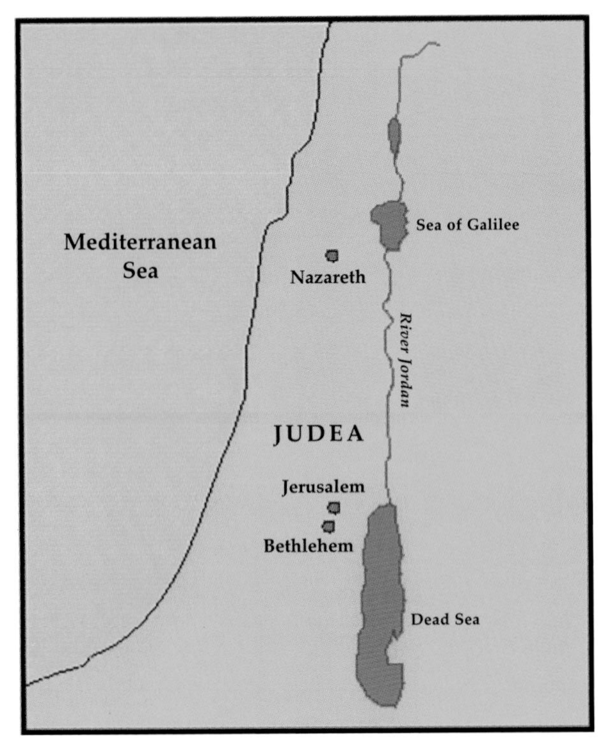

Palestine at the time of Jesus

IORI Jesus was a Jew. In the Jewish religion, there has always been a belief that God will send a wonderful person, the **Messiah**, to save the world from everything which is bad. The **prophets** in the **Bible** talked about the Messiah and how he would bring peace to the earth. Some of the things they said about the Messiah are like some of the stories about the birth of Jesus. For example, they said that the Messiah would be related to King David and would be born in Bethlehem.

Christians believe that Jesus was the Messiah. Most of the first Christians were Jews who believed that at last the Messiah had arrived. Because they were followers of the Messiah, or the **Christ**, they became known as "Christians".

Iori: *Jesus was crucified by the Romans, like thousands of others.*

THINK ABOUT:

Christians believe that Jesus did wonderful things. If someone with amazing powers lived today, what would you want this person to do with those powers?

What did the Jews believe about the Messiah? Why do you think some people who knew Jesus believed he was the Messiah?

Does it matter what Jesus looked like?

REBECCA Christianity started with Jesus about 2,000 years ago. The greatest thing to us is following the word of Jesus Christ – what he said in the Bible. Some people think Jesus was soft and gentle but he had to be really strong. He stood up to anyone he thought was wrong, like the time he went into the Temple in Jerusalem and overturned the market stalls.

It was because Jesus spoke out against the leaders of the time that they wanted him put to death. He was put on trial and then **crucified**. But of course the story didn't end there. Christianity really began after Jesus was put to death because, as Christians, we believe that he came back to life again.

FACT FILE

Messiah A messenger sent from God; Messiah means "the chosen one".

Prophet Someone who speaks on behalf of God. In the Bible a prophet often spoke out against the way people of the time behaved and warned how God would punish them.

Bible The holy book for Christians. It is divided into two parts, the Old Testament and the New Testament. It is this second part which deals with the life and teachings of Jesus and records the story of the first Christians.

Christ The Greek word for Messiah.

Crucified A person was crucified by being tied or nailed to a wooden cross and then left to die. The Romans used to punish people this way 2,000 years ago.

Rebecca: *In the Bible there are several stories about Jesus being seen after he came back to life.*

THINGS TO DO

What sort of person was Jesus? Draw a human outline and inside write words which could describe Jesus, from what you know about him.

Make a copy of the map of Palestine at the time of Jesus. Write a sentence about each of the following places to say what important events in Jesus' life took place there: Bethlehem, Nazareth, Jerusalem, the River Jordan. (Clue: look in the Index.)

Jesus was ready to die for what he believed in. Is anything worth dying for? Write down your views on this question.

How my religion began: Christianity grows

Rebecca: St Peter's Church in Rome has a huge square where Catholics gather to listen to the Pope.

Think about:

What was the one thing which made the first Christians start preaching to other people?

Why didn't the first Christians have special buildings to meet in?

How many different churches or denominations are mentioned in this book? Do you think it is a good thing that there are lots of different Christian churches?

DAVINIA Jesus spent most of his life in Nazareth. He didn't start **preaching** until the last two or three years of his life and then he gained many followers. If nothing else had happened after he was crucified and buried, the story would have ended there. But it didn't. Jesus rose from the dead, he came back to life.

REBECCA If the followers of Jesus hadn't believed that he rose from the dead, they would just have remembered him as a good man. But God gave his **disciples** the strength to go out and spread the message that Jesus was alive across the whole world. That's the meaning of the word Catholic – world-wide, over the whole world. The disciple named Peter went to Rome and started a church there. That's how my church came to be called the Roman Catholic Church.

IORI The first Christians tried to live simple lives, sharing what they had and worshipping together. They used to meet in each others' houses because there were no churches at the time. In some places they were being picked on and even put to death for being Christians. A man called Paul used to **persecute** Christians until, one day, he felt that Jesus spoke to him. From then on he became a Christian and helped to spread Christianity. He wrote several of the books now found in the Bible.

Iori: Some of the first Christians in Rome had to meet in secret, sometimes in these underground passages where the dead were buried.

Iori: Many of the ruined monasteries we see today were Catholic and were destroyed when Henry set up his own church.

Fact File

Preaching Speaking to people to spread a message about God.

Disciples Followers or pupils, people who learn from and believe in a teacher. Jesus had 12 close disciples who are mentioned by name in the Bible.

Persecute To pick on someone or a group of people. The early Christians were persecuted by the Romans and often tortured or put to death.

My church, the Church in Wales, and the Church of England used to be one community. Before that we all used to be part of the Roman Catholic Church. It was King Henry the Eighth who started the Church of England when he disagreed with the Pope in Rome. I think it's good that there are lots of different sorts of churches.

RUTH In 1865 a man called William Booth started to preach about God to the poor people in the East End of London. He had a hard time and was often attacked. Enough people listened to his message and saw that he didn't just talk but really helped them. In 1878 he began to use the name "The Salvation Army". By the time General Booth died in 1912, the Army was at work in 58 countries.

Ruth: General William Booth preached to hundreds of people at a time.

Things to do

Look in a copy of the Bible and count how many of Paul's letters are to be found there. Draw a bookshelf with the right number of books on it, one for each letter. Write on the spine of the book the name of the people to whom each letter was sent. Or you could use real envelopes to write the names of the people on and make a display of them.

Design a poster which General Booth and his Salvation Army might have used to spread their message.

Write a story about someone, or a group of people, being persecuted. It could be about the early Christians if you wish.

Starting out: welcoming the baby

THINK ABOUT:

Why is the birth of a new baby an event which many people celebrate?

What different ways are there to welcome someone?

What are godparents? How might they help children as they grow up?

DAVINIA We welcome a new baby into the family of the church. We pray for the baby and sing songs like "Jesus loves me, this I know". We don't put water on the baby, but just pray for it and ask for it to be blessed. The baby is given its full name and a certificate.

My youngest sister, Michaela, was just over three months old when we took her to be welcomed. Lots of our family came, some even came from London. The church was packed with all our family, the godparents and a big **congregation**. Afterwards we had a big party.

First the godparents held Michaela, then the **Pastor** did. She needs godparents to look after her in case anything happens to Mum and Dad. My godparents are Lester, Tina and Colin. I still keep in touch with them and they sometimes give me some money.

***Davinia:** When I was welcomed into the church they gave me presents – a Bible and a dish with a spoon.*

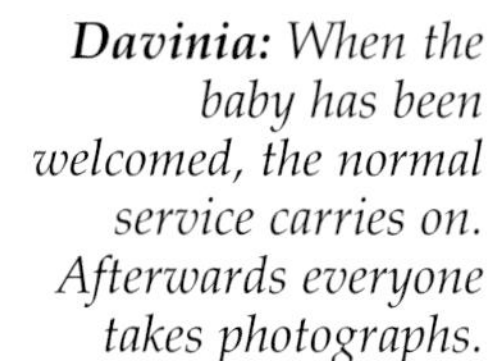

***Davinia:** When the baby has been welcomed, the normal service carries on. Afterwards everyone takes photographs.*

RUTH When a baby is a few weeks old there is a **dedication** during one of our services. The **officer** blesses the child and asks God to look after it. We don't have a font or a baptism but the baby is given its full name in a dedication prayer. The mother and father take part, and the godparents. They all go up the front onto the platform and the Army flag is held up at the back. We pray that the baby will live a good life as a Christian.

FACT FILE

Congregation The people who attend a church.

Pastor The name given to the leader in some churches.

Dedication Giving over to God's care.

Officer The leader of a Salvation Army Corps.

Davinia: We like to celebrate the arrival of a new baby into our church with special food.

THINGS TO DO

Draw a card of welcome for a new-born baby. On it include pictures of two presents which the baby might want to keep when he or she is older.

What sort of life would you want a baby born today to have? Write a prayer or a poem about the life that you hope a new baby can look forward to.

It is a big responsibility looking after a baby. What do you think are the most important things to give a child? Write a paragraph explaining your ideas.

Starting out: infant baptism

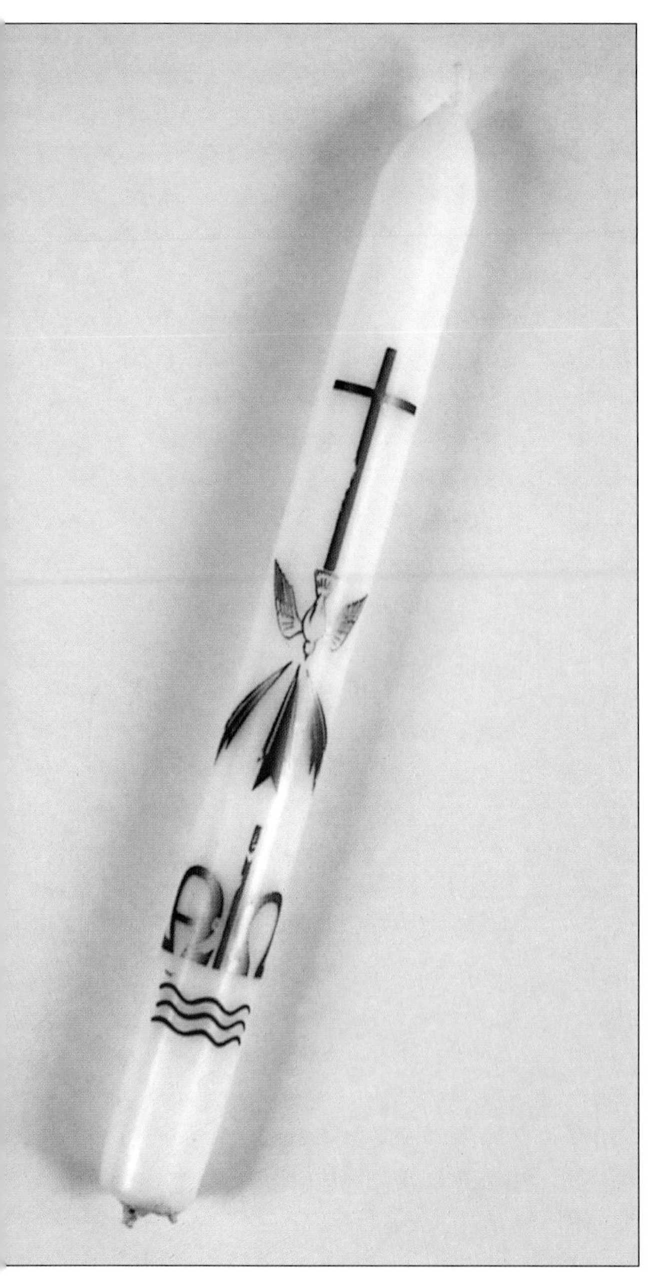

***Rebecca:** The baptismal candle is lit from the Easter candle to pass on the new life which Jesus gave us. You can also see a symbol on the candle to represent the water.*

SIONED A baby is baptised as part of our normal Sunday service. The **minister** holds the baby and puts water on his forehead in the shape of a cross. The water is in a small bowl at the front. The minister says that the baby is then part of the chapel. Baptism marks the starting point of a person's life in the Christian family. When my nephew was baptised the whole family was there.

REBECCA In our church Mam and Dad and the godparents first have to say the **creed** out loud. The priest then says a prayer to ask for a good life for the baby. Water is poured over the baby's head and the priest says:

I baptise you in the name of the Father and of the Son and of the Holy Spirit. Amen.

The idea of the water is very important. It shows that the baby is making a clean start to its life. The water is in the **font** which is near to the door. It is nice seeing another member coming into the Catholic family.

There is a candle called the Easter candle in our church. Another candle is lit from this and given to a godparent. It reminds us of Jesus' new life after he died and then came back from the dead. My sister, Anna, has been asked to be godmother to a friend's baby. She will have to help the child to know God and grow up in the church.

Parents choose the baby's name. My name and Anna's come from the Bible. I like both our names and knowing that they come from the Bible is even better.

THINK ABOUT:

Why are babies baptised in some Christian churches?

Why might the font be near the main door of a church?

Rebecca describes a candle being lit at an infant baptism. A candle flame behaves almost as if it is alive. What do you think of when you look at a candle flame? Why might people at a baptism like to look at a lit candle?

FACT FILE

Minister The name given to the leader in many churches.

Creed A statement saying what someone believes about God.

Font A stone basin used for baptisms, usually found inside the main entrance of a church.

Rebecca: *A baptism is a happy, family occasion.*

Sioned: *Some people like to send cards if they cannot get to the baptism.*

THINGS TO DO

Design a card to celebrate an infant baptism. Include on it the candle and the water. Make up suitable words as part of your design.

Write an advert to go in the local paper to announce the birth of a new baby. Write it as if you were a Christian and wanted to say how glad you were to have this wonderful gift from God.

Do any children in your class or school have names which are found in the Bible? Make a list of those which you think are Bible names. Use your school library to look up three of the names and write a short piece about each one.

Following the path

Ruth: *The four Gospels are a very small but very important part of the whole Bible.*

RUTH Christianity started with Jesus Christ. It is very important to us to follow the word of Jesus. The things which he said are written down in the Bible. There are lots of books in the Bible but only four of those books are just about Jesus' life. They were written by four different people, Matthew, Mark, Luke and John. These books are known as the four **Gospels**. We also try to follow the **Ten Commandments** which were written over 1,000 years before Jesus.

I sometimes read the Bible. Mum or Dad don't tell me I've got to, but sometimes I do. I'll do this if I feel low or upset, then it seems to help. I haven't really got any favourite passages.

PHILIPPA The Bible is very important in our house. There's a copy in all the rooms: in the kitchen, the study, the computer room, in my bedroom, other people's rooms, on the stereo, on the shelves, everywhere! We all have our own Bibles.

SIONED I read parts of the Bible at Sunday School. The Bible is difficult to read so we have books which are written for children and they make the Bible easier to understand. In the church itself the Bible is in the most important place – right at the front in the middle.

Philippa: *We sometimes read the Bible together as a family.*

THINK ABOUT:

Why are the Gospels "good news" for Christians?

The four Gospels contain some information which is exactly the same and some which is different. Why might this be?

What are the different ways in which Ruth, Philippa and Sioned use the Bible?

Sioned: *We will usually have a story read to us at Sunday School but sometimes I like to choose a book for myself from the library there.*

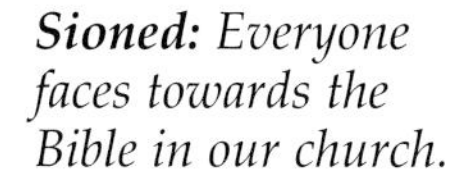

Sioned: *Everyone faces towards the Bible in our church.*

FACT FILE

Gospel means “good news”. The first Christians preached about and then wrote down the good news about Jesus’ life.

Ten Commandments Ten laws given to Moses. They say how people should behave towards God and each other.

Lectern A reading stand, often in the shape of an eagle standing on a globe. The Bible is placed on the outstretched wings to show that God’s message should be carried across the world.

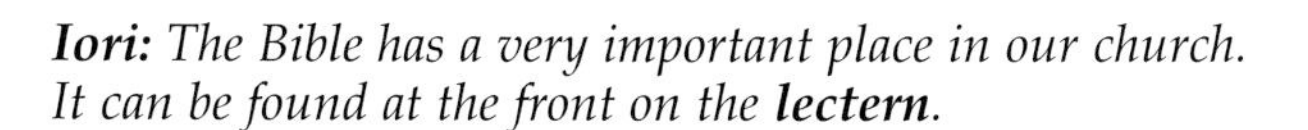

Iori: *The Bible has a very important place in our church. It can be found at the front on the* ***lectern****.*

THINGS TO DO

Design a book cover for one of the four Gospels. Write on it the name of the Gospel and decorate it to show its importance. You could work in a group of four to do one each for a display.

The eagle is a common design for a lectern. Design your own lectern using a different idea. Think about how, for Christians, it is meant to carry something very important, the word of God.

Look up the Ten Commandments in the Bible. You will find them in the Book of Exodus chapter 20 verses 2 to 17 (or ask if your teacher has them on a separate sheet). Pick out the three which you think are the most important. Write them out very neatly and underneath each one say what happens if people don’t follow this rule.

Following the path: stories in the Bible

Rebecca: *We remember the story of Jesus riding into Jerusalem by holding up small crosses on Palm Sunday.*

REBECCA I have learnt about Jesus from my family, the church and the Bible – these are the important three. My Bible is *The Children's Bible* and I've read it over and over again. I like it all. My favourite story is the beginning of the Easter story when Jesus rode a donkey into **Jerusalem**. Everyone waved palm leaves and laid them down on the road in front of him. It must have been really exciting, welcoming someone like that who you thought was very special.

PHILIPPA In the Bible I like reading about the **miracles** Jesus did. It says in John's Gospel that he turned water into wine. He also fed 5,000 people with five loaves and two fishes. Jesus did miracles to show he was a real person who cared about other people. But the miracles he did also show he was God's Son.

THINK ABOUT:

Why is it important for Christians to know the story of Jesus' life?

Is there a book which you have read many times over? Why is it so special to you?

What questions would you want to ask about the story of the feeding of the 5,000? Are they questions which have easy answers?

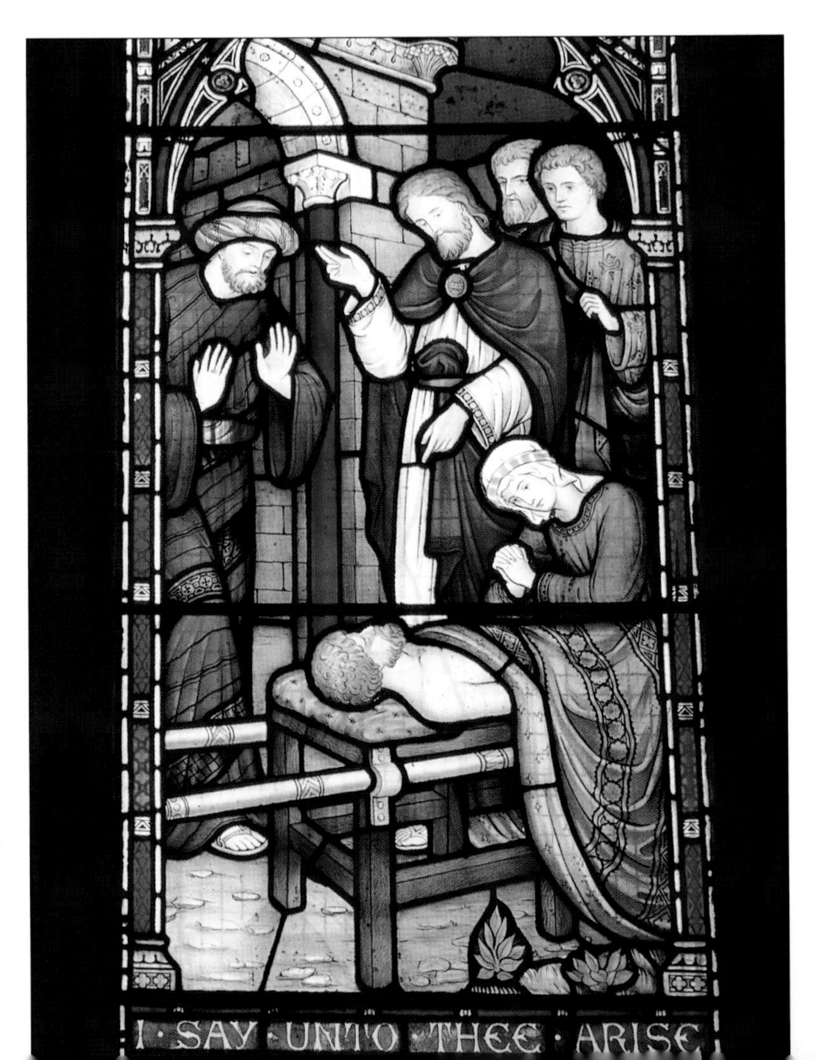

Philippa: *I like the miracle story when the friends of a paralysed man took him to Jesus to be healed.*

IORI I have been brought up as a Christian and told stories from the Bible. I believe the Bible is true up to a point. Certain things must have happened. I am sure that Jesus lived, he was a preacher and helped people. But I am not sure about believing all the miracles. This does not affect my faith in God though.

FACT FILE

Jerusalem The capital city of the country where Jesus lived. He was put to death just outside Jerusalem.

Miracle A wonderful event or something which science finds difficult to explain.

Fishing today in the Sea of Galilee. The fish are called Peter fish.

THINGS TO DO

Read the story of the feeding of the 5,000 again. Tell the story in your words as if you were someone in the crowd. Say what you think happened, what you felt at the time and what you thought of Jesus.

The Bible contains many stories which help Christians in their lives. Tell a story of your own which you think has an important message for people to follow.

Some people believe that miracles still happen today. Even everyday things like the birth of a new baby can sometimes seem like a miracle. Look through newspapers and magazines to find examples of wonderful or amazing things that have happened. Cut out the picture or story, paste it onto paper and write a few sentences next to it to say why you have chosen it.

What we believe

IORI Belief is a very personal thing. You can't tell someone what to believe and what not to believe. Basically it's down to your own faith. There are some things to do with Christianity that I don't believe but I think there is a life after death and that Jesus did rise from the dead, somehow. It happened so long ago that you aren't going to find any proof. I don't always know quite why I believe what I do.

PHILIPPA Jesus died on the cross to take our sins away. It's like when you do things wrong and someone lets you off. You feel so relieved and it's a weight off your shoulders. Anybody can be saved if they want to be. You have to follow Jesus and believe that he died on the cross and rose again from the dead.

REBECCA We also believe in the Holy Spirit. It's very difficult to describe. It's like the power of God doing good here on earth. One of our friends has a daughter called Helen who is in a wheel chair. We were all in a prayer meeting and a woman said, "Christ is walking in our midst." Everybody stopped and said, "Look at Helen!" She was smiling the most beautiful smile. It touched us to see her in her wheel chair. It's at times like that when you understand what the Holy Spirit does.

***Rebecca:** The Holy Spirit is a bit like the wind – you can't see it but you can see what it does.*

THINK ABOUT:

What is the difference between a fact and a belief?

What do you believe in? Where do your beliefs come from?

Christians talk about Jesus as someone who is very special. What do Christians believe about Jesus?

***Iori:** I believe that Jesus showed us there can be a life after death, such as when he brought a little girl back to life.*

THINGS TO DO

Use a dictionary to find out what "faith" means. Write three sentences using the word "faith", to show you understand what it means.

Christians believe that the Holy Spirit is a powerful force which does good in the world. Make a poster using combinations of words, pictures and colour to suggest those invisible forces which bring good to the world. (Some ideas to think about: warmth, love, courage.)

What sorts of things do you believe and not believe?
Can you always give a reason for what you believe?
Make two lists, then discuss your lists with a friend:

Things I believe	Things I don't believe

Philippa: *There are some things which just can't be explained. You just feel good about them or know they are true.*

What we believe about God

Philippa: *God made a beautiful world, if only we would look after it.*

IORI I believe in God partly because of the way I have been brought up and partly because I have a feeling that there is more to life than science can tell us.

PHILIPPA I think I'll see God in heaven but I don't know what God is like. We have this discussion in school about what you think God looks like. I don't know if it really matters what God looks like, if he looks like anything. I do believe that God made the world. It's amazing that God made the world but we've mucked it up.

DAVINIA I believe God is there and he loves us. In church people pray to God and sing to him. They are showing what they think of him, how much they love him. When I was younger, I used to think that he was a man above the clouds with a white beard and white long hair. He used to have a little game board in front of him. We were like people on the game board. He would move us around and put the ideas in our heads.

Now I think God is invisible, you can't see him. In a way I still think he knows what we are going to do before we do it. I think God's got everything planned out. It doesn't mean that God plans for people to be bad, we have some choices.

THINK ABOUT:

Do you think that we will ever know everything there is to know? Will science answer all our questions?

Davinia's ideas about God have changed as she has grown older. Have your ideas about God changed? How?

Does it matter whether people think of God as male or female?

Davinia: *My ideas about God have changed, as many children's do.*

Ruth: You can't see God. He is all around us though.

RUTH God – I believe he's there. He is real. I believe that he created the world and that his son is Jesus. I don't know why I think of God as a he. I've always been told that God is a he so I've just got used to calling God "he" and "him". I couldn't describe God. God isn't **physical**, God makes you **spiritual**.

FACT FILE

Physical Made up of things which can be seen and touched.

Spiritual To do with feelings and beliefs, and things which are not physical. Religious people believe that a person's spirit is the gift of life from God which makes us more than just a collection of flesh and bones.

THINGS TO DO

Many Christians believe you cannot really draw a picture of God in the same way that you can of a person. But you can say what God is like. On a piece of plain paper write down different words which you think help to say what God is like. These may be your own ideas of God or Christian ideas.

Philippa believes that God made the world but humans have made a mess of it. Do you agree with her? Write out your answer giving reasons for your views.

Make up a list of questions to ask friends about their beliefs about God. Ask questions which can mostly be answered "Yes" or "No" or "Unsure". You could, as a homework, ask friends and family outside of school too. Write up your results saying what you have found out. If you can, use the computer to produce the answers in the form of graphs.

Right and wrong

RUTH I do things that are wrong. I suppose everyone does. I have been taught what's right and wrong by Mum and Dad, by teachers at school and by Sunday School teachers. When I've done something wrong I know because I can feel it. If I do something wrong I apologise. If I am **tempted** to do something wrong I try to remember to do the right thing.

PHILIPPA Sin is when you do things that are wrong. Things like fighting, swearing, cheating, or being cheeky to your parents. You should listen to your parents. You shouldn't disobey them. If they've told me to wash and I say "No!", I upset my mum. It's not right. If I have been unkind to someone I'll say sorry. I say sorry to God first.

Ruth: *I might pray if I've done something really bad. I would ask to be forgiven and then I believe that I am forgiven.*

Philippa: *Our teacher at Sunday School sets us a good example and we learn to help each other.*

THINK ABOUT:

How have you learnt right from wrong? Who do you pay most attention to when being told what is right or wrong?

What sorts of things are you tempted to do, but know you should not do? How do you decide whether to do them or not?

Forgiveness is a very important part of Christian belief. Is it easy to forgive? Jesus said that people should forgive others every time they do wrong. Do you agree?

Sioned: I try to do as my mam says but we don't always agree what time I should be home.

Fact File

Tempted Invited to do something which you know is wrong. You can be tempted by your own thoughts as well as by another person.

SIONED Some children in school are rude to the teachers. I'm not perfect, anyone will tell you that, but I try not to do bad things. I don't do bad things deliberately. It's not easy when my parents want me to do one thing and I want to do another.

DAVINIA Rules help you decide what's right and wrong. The rule in the Ten Commandments says that you shouldn't steal. Our Pastor said if you are in a situation where you don't know what to do you should ask yourself, "What would Jesus do?", and use that as a guide.

Things to do

Choose one of the things in this chapter which a Christian talks about as being right or wrong. Make a poster which will remind children about this.

Write a story about someone who was tempted to do something wrong. Make sure there is a beginning, middle and end. Try to show what the person who is being tempted is thinking.

Write a set of rules all about doing what is right. You are NOT allowed to use the words "Not", "Never" or "No".

Putting things right with God

RUTH During our service you can, if you want, go down to the Mercy Seat and someone will come and pray with you. The Mercy Seat is the long seat at the front of the hall and it's where you can have time to yourself and pray. It's usually got a Bible open on it. You can go up at any time during the service. People don't often go up.

On a Junior Soldiers' Sunday the **Promise Renewal** cards are laid out on the Mercy Seat so you go up to the Mercy Seat to sign the Promise. The Army Promise reminds me of what not to do, like swear, drink alcohol, smoke. It also has other rules to say what we should do, like to pray, read your Bible, help others, to follow Jesus.

Ruth: *If you go to the Mercy Seat someone will usually come and pray, or read the Bible, with you.*

THINK ABOUT:

What is the Mercy Seat for in Ruth's church?

Why do people find it hard to confess or own up when they have done something wrong? Should you always own up when you have done something wrong?

How do you think Rebecca feels when she has been to confession?

THE SALVATION ARMY
United Kingdom
Territory

MY PROMISE

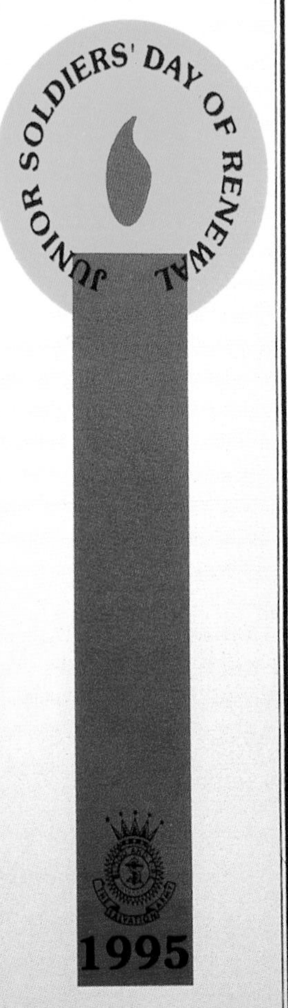

Having asked God for forgiveness, I will be his loving and obedient child.

Because Jesus is my Saviour from sin, I will trust him to keep me good, and will try to help others to follow him.

I promise to pray, to read my Bible and, by his help, to lead a life that is clean in thought, word and deed.

Today I renew my promise.

Signed

Ruth Davies

30th of April 95 (date)

You are like light for the whole world...

Your light must shine before people, so that they will see the good things you do and praise your Father in heaven.

Matthew 5:14-16 (TEV)

Ruth: *Signing the Promise is making a promise to myself and a promise to God.*

Rebecca: *I pray in church for forgiveness, but I'm sure God hears you wherever you are.*

FACT FILE

Promise Renewal A certificate setting out what a Junior Soldier believes and the promises he or she makes to God. It is signed every year to renew the promise.

Confession Owning up to something that you have done wrong.

REBECCA I try to put things right when I say a prayer at night. I will ask Jesus to forgive me. Then I say to myself, "Rebecca, don't do it again." I can go to **confession** at church when the priest listens to me talk about what I have done wrong. I'm not sure what I confessed the first time. Sometimes you have to think hard to know what you have done. If I have lost my temper and shouted at my sister I might confess that. Jesus then forgives me and the priest tells me to pray.

Rebecca: *In some Catholic churches when you go to confess, you kneel in front of a curtain. The priest, who is on the other side, listens to your confession.*

THINGS TO DO

Look up what the word "Mercy" means. Write a short story in which someone shows mercy.

Write a prayer or a poem about asking for forgiveness.

Everyone does something which is wrong sometimes. Write a list of five things which many people do that are wrong. Next to each one write what they could do to put them right.

Wrong	Putting it right
1.	

Daily life at home

Ruth: Being together as a family means a lot to us.

RUTH We usually say prayers at meal times and if you want you can say your own prayers at bed time or any other time. I wouldn't say there is anything which we really have to do every day to follow our religion. If a stranger came into our house they might be able to tell that we are Christians, but more by how we behave than anything they would see. We base our lives on what the Bible says.

IORI If you came into my bedroom you would see masses of football posters, books and magazines but amongst them one **crucifix** and an **icon**. I have two Bibles but they are mostly used as book-ends to hold up an enormous collection of adventure game books.

DAVINIA At home I have to keep my room clean and do washing up, which I don't like. My mum likes me to come straight in from school so she knows where I am. She also has a rule about what time I have to go to bed in the week but at weekends I try to stay up as late as I can. I pray before I go to bed.

We have to be honest with our families and our neighbours. You have to treat other people as you would like them to treat you, be like the **Good Samaritan**. There are no rules in our religion about food or clothes but most of the women wear hats to our church.

***Ruth:** Our Home League banner shows that we should try to base our lives at home on what the Bible teaches.*

THINK ABOUT:

What rules are there in your house? What is the point of those rules?

Many Christians believe that it is important for a family to have meals together. Why do you think this is? How often do you have family meals? Do you prefer eating together or on your own?

If a stranger came to your home what could they tell about you and your family from what they saw around the house?

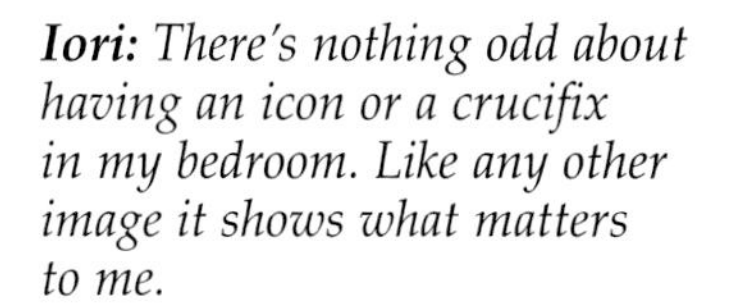

***Iori:** There's nothing odd about having an icon or a crucifix in my bedroom. Like any other image it shows what matters to me.*

Fact file

Crucifix A cross with Jesus on, showing how he suffered when he was crucified.

Icon A religious picture often used to help a Christian pray. Many icons show Mary holding Jesus as a baby.

Good Samaritan A character in one of the stories Jesus told. He was someone from Samaria who helped an injured Jew even though the Jews and Samaritans were enemies.

Things to do

Look through the book to find pictures which show Christians at home. What can you see which tells you that they are Christians? Draw one of the objects or actions and label it.

Make a picture of your own in the style of an icon. You could use silver foil, paper, colours, paint and other materials.

Christians try to live their daily lives based on their beliefs. What do you believe which affects your daily life? Complete a day's diary below to show how your beliefs affect your life. This one is started as if Davinia were filling it in.

Diary	Belief
Monday	
7.00 Get up, get washed and dressed.	*Must stay clean.*
7.20 Say grace. Have toast and drink.	*Proper breakfast will keep me going. Thank God for food.*
8.30 Leave for school.	*It's polite to be on time. School is important.*

Life outside the home

Philippa: *Wearing the badge is a way of saying, "I am a Christian." You're not ashamed of letting other people know.*

PHILIPPA Once a week all the Christians in school meet together at lunch time. One of the science teachers organises the meetings. We have people come to talk to us and we have Bible study. Sometimes people at school laugh at you just because you are a Christian. Some pupils don't mind and will wear badges, like the **fish symbol** or a cross, to show they are Christian.

REBECCA Being a Christian means you sometimes have to make hard choices. For example a lot of young people smoke. They don't seem to care who they upset or what harm they do to themselves. God gave us the power to decide things for ourselves. If someone offered me a cigarette I would choose not to take it. You must stick to what you believe is right, even if it means standing up to other people.

THINK ABOUT:

Do you think about what you do and what you say before you do and say it?

Why do people wear badges? What badges do you wear?

What do you think of people who laugh at others for what they believe? How might Christians feel when that happens?

Rebecca: *Some Christian women give their whole life to God by becoming nuns. They wear special clothes as a sign of the choice they have made. In this picture, can you see what makes the nun's clothes special?*

Ruth: At church or out in town with the band, our uniform says who we are.

FACT FILE

Fish symbol A simple drawing of a fish. It was used first by early Christians as a secret sign. The first two letters of the Greek word for fish are also the two initial letters for Jesus Christ.

Salvation Being saved from doing wrong things and given a new life.

RUTH If you're a Junior Soldier and in the Sing Company or the Young People's Band, then you have to wear uniform on Sundays. Otherwise if you don't want to wear the uniform you don't have to. The tie is red, yellow and blue. Yellow is for the fire of the Holy Spirit, blue is for the pure goodness of God, like pure water, and red is the blood. The blood is because Jesus died for us and it reminds us of when he died and why he died. The badge shows the cross on which Jesus died. It has a big S which stands for **Salvation**.

DAVINIA In church we are taught that Christians should be good at all times, not just Sundays. That isn't always easy. There are rules at school I should follow, but don't. You are not supposed to chew in class but I do.

THINGS TO DO

Draw the fish and cross symbols. Next to each one write down what it means to Christians. Look at page 12 to remind yourself why some early Christians had to use secret signs.

Design a poster to advertise the Christian group which meets at Philippa's school.

Write about a time when you had to stand up for what you believed was right, even though you might have suffered because of it.

There are many different symbols which Christians might wear as badges.

Growing up: baptism

***Philippa:** The two people baptised with me were much older. We sang and prayed first.*

PHILIPPA In our church you can only be baptised when you are old enough to decide for yourself. My sister, Laura, was baptised when she was ten. We are taught that we should be baptised because Jesus was baptised in the River Jordan by John the Baptist. Before being baptised I went to classes to learn about what it means to be a Christian.

I wrote my **testimony** before the service. I then read it out in front of the congregation to say why I had become a Christian. The pool is at the front of the church and I went down the steps into the water. Geraint, our minister, baptised me by tipping me backwards right under the water and then lifting me out again. We all felt really happy afterwards. I've changed in some ways. I used to swear a lot, but not any more.

THINK ABOUT:

Why wasn't Philippa baptised as a baby?

How do you think Philippa felt at her baptism? Is it easy talking about yourself in front of lots of other people?

Why does the person go right under the water in the sort of baptism which Philippa chose?

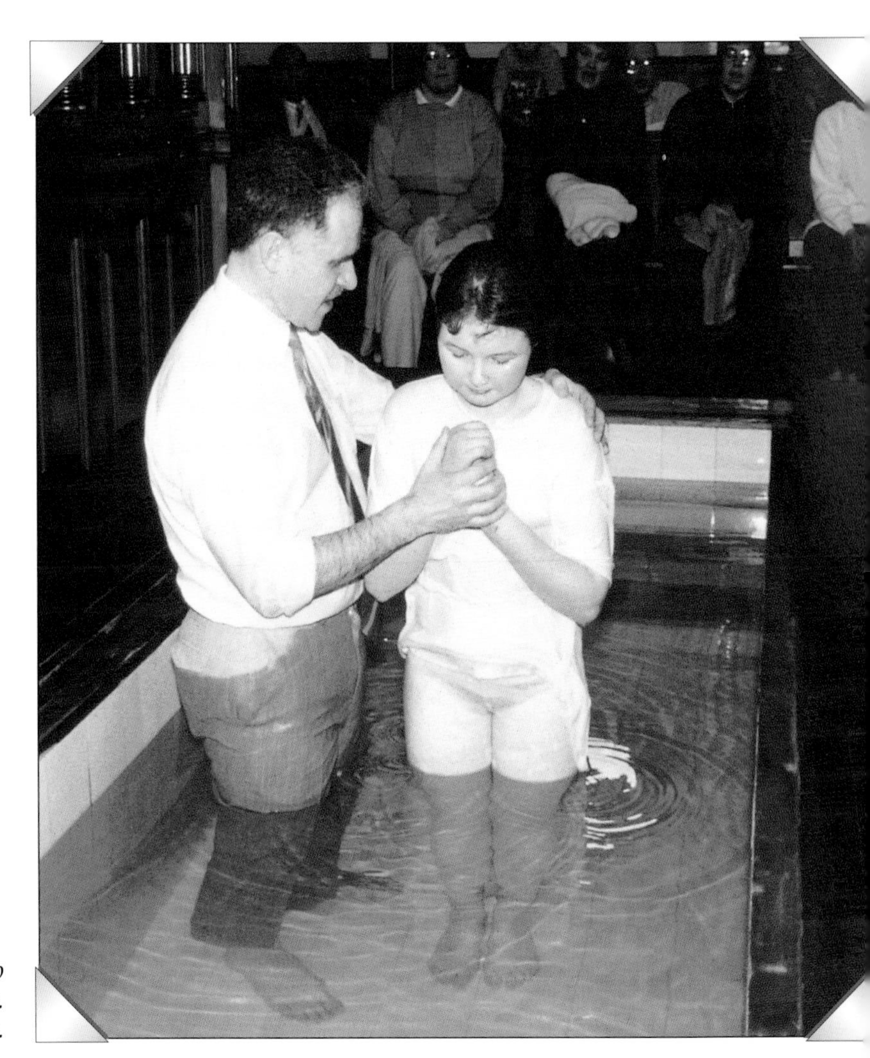

***Philippa:** Going under the water is to show that we are starting a new life. You die and you rise again, like Jesus.*

Davinia: None of my friends has been baptised yet, neither have I. I want to learn as much as I can about my religion before making the decision.

Fact File

Testimony A statement to say something which you believe is true and want to tell others about.

Vow A promise.

Lord A common term for Jesus and God. For a Christian it puts over the belief that God is like a ruler who guides a person's life.

DAVINIA When you are baptised and make that **vow** to be a good Christian, it is a commitment for life, no matter what you come up against. At the baptism you give a testimony and say what you were like before, how you came to know the **Lord** and how it has changed you. You make a promise, in front of family and friends, about how you are going to serve the Lord from now on.

Things to do

Imagine what it would be like if you were under water for more than a few seconds. Perhaps you have done this when swimming at the seaside. Make a list of the words you could use to describe being under the water for a while. Then make another list of what it is like to come up out of the water and into the sunshine. Colour in two halves of a piece of paper to show being under water and being out in the air and sun. Write the words from your two lists onto the correct parts of the paper.

When making a testimony, people think very deeply about what they believe to be true and want others to know about. Write about something that you feel is really important and want to tell others about.

If you were going to change some things about yourself, what would they be? You can answer this by copying the chart below and filling it in. An example is done for you – you can use it if it's true!

Me now	Me as I would like to be	Reason for changing
I talk too much	*A much better listener*	*I would do better at school*

Growing up: making promises

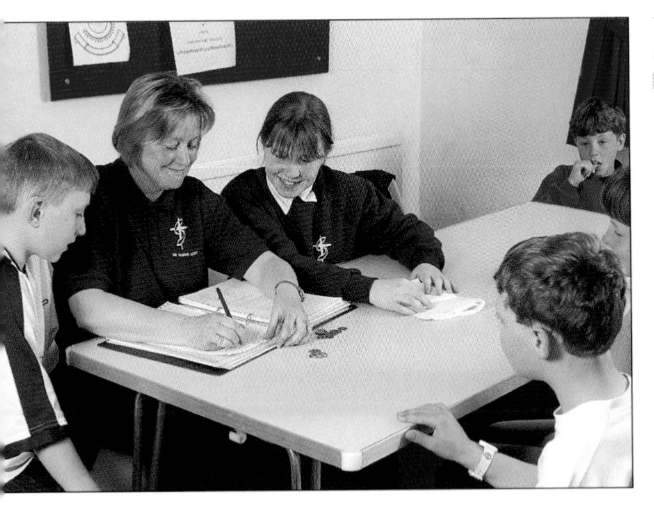

Ruth: Lots of young people come along to the Sunday School. I help to keep the register.

RUTH Before you become a Junior Soldier you have lessons every week. At the end you sign a certificate and say a promise. I was seven when I did this but it can be any age. You decide for yourself to go through this. You make your promise in the hall at a Sunday service. When you become a Junior Soldier you can start to wear the uniform and join the Young People's Band and Sing Company, which is the choir. It's good being in the Sing Company and you get to see your friends on a Tuesday when we practise. From the age of 14 you can become a Senior Soldier. I don't think I will when I'm 14 because it's too young, but perhaps later on.

REBECCA A big step for Catholic children is having first communion when we are seven. We have lessons on how to take the communion because at seven it isn't easy to understand what communion is. I really looked forward to my first communion.

Rebecca: This was me dressed up for my first communion.

THINK ABOUT:

What does Ruth enjoy about being a Junior Soldier? What groups have you joined? What do you enjoy about belonging to them?

Why do some churches have confirmation? If you were being given a confirmation present, what do you think you would value most in twenty years time – a cross on a chain or a television set?

What do you think Rebecca means when she says she will be "stronger" when she is 13? Think about the different ways in which people can be strong.

When we are 12 we can be confirmed by the **bishop.** At her confirmation, my sister Anna made promises to God to turn away from evil and follow the ways of Jesus. I'd like to be confirmed when I'm 13. I'll be stronger then. When children have first communion or confirmation, people buy them sweets or little crosses or a prayer book.

IORI Confirmation is making sure what you believe. You go to classes with the vicar to learn what is expected of you, the sort of life you should lead. The bishop comes to your church for your confirmation. You have to renew the promises made for you when you were baptised as a baby.

Rebecca: *Anna had her picture taken with the bishop after her confirmation.*

Iori: *At confirmation you kneel in front of the bishop. He lays his hands on your head and says a prayer.*

Things to do

Draw two things you would like to have as presents to mark a special time in your life as you grow up.

Think about a time when you made an important promise. Tell the story of why you made the promise. What was the promise? What happened after you had made it?

Draw an outline of yourself. In it write the different ways in which you are strong now. Draw a second outline of yourself as a grown-up. In it, write the ways you think you will be strong when you are an adult.

Fact File

Bishop A bishop is someone in authority who has care of the churches in his area. Not all Christian denominations have bishops.

Worship in the home

DAVINIA Our family all pray together every morning before we go to school or work and one of us reads the **scriptures**. When my dad is home we have a service in the mornings. My mum opens our windows when she is playing **gospel music** so the neighbours can hear. I pray before I go to bed in case anything happens to me. I say the **Lord's Prayer** and one I learnt at school:

Lord keep us safe this night,
Secure from all our fears.
May angels guard us in our sleep,
Till morning light appears. Amen.

In my own prayer I say, "Thank you God for waking me up this morning, and for keeping me and my family safe. Thank you for my family." When I had my viola exam I was worried and I prayed that I would pass and do well.

IORI I sort of pray daily. There is no set pattern of prayer I follow every day but sometimes I might want to discuss something with God. It depends on what sort of mood I'm in. We have **grace** before lunch or a main meal but not before breakfast.

THINK ABOUT:

Why does Davinia's mum want to share the gospel music with her neighbours? Are there things which you really want to share with others?

What different reasons have Davinia, Iori and Rebecca given for praying?

Iori says he "discusses things with God." What do you think he means?

Rebecca: *One of us rolls a dice which has six prayers on, in German. We then all say the prayer which comes up.*

Rebecca: Praying means a lot to me. When I use the rosary I close my eyes and think about what Jesus has been through.

REBECCA

When we come home, we pray. That's something to look forward to in our lives. We pray at meal times mostly, but also in the night. We use the rosary, which is a string of beads, to help us pray. We count through the beads and it reminds us of what happened in the life of Jesus and Mary. We also say the **Hail Mary**.

THINGS TO DO

The families of Davinia, Iori and Rebecca each worship together every day. They feel this brings them close together as a family. Draw a picture or write a story with the title "The family together". It should show your own ideas of what brings a family together.

Design a chain of beads that would help you remember things that are important to you. Draw the beads, and perhaps other small symbols, tied onto a thread. Does the colour of the thread and beads matter? Explain what your chain means. If you have the materials you could make your chain of beads.

Write your own prayer of thanks or a prayer of thanks which a Christian might use.

FACT FILE

Scriptures simply means "writings". For Christians it is another word for the Bible.

Gospel music Popular songs praising God and Jesus.

Lord's Prayer The prayer Jesus taught his disciples, beginning "Our Father ..."

Grace A prayer of thanks often said before meals.

Hail Mary A prayer to Mary, praising her as the mother of Jesus.

Worshipping together 1

Rebecca: Something very special happens when the priest blesses the bread and wine.

REBECCA I've been told that before our church was built we used to meet in a school or in someone's house and have Mass there. When we go into the church for a service we make a sign of the cross with **holy water**. That reminds us we are in God's house now and that it's important to think about God. The most important part of the service is the **Eucharist**. That is when we remember Jesus dying. The wine stands for his blood and the bread is his body.

What surprised us when we went out to Germany to see Dad's family was the way they prayed. They weren't embarrassed to pray. You would go for a walk out in the forest and see people go up to an **altar** that you would find in the middle of the forest and just pray.

THINK ABOUT:

Is it necessary for Christians to meet in a church or chapel to worship?

Do people behave differently inside churches? In what ways? Why do you think this is?

Why do Iori and Rebecca go to church?

Iori: Sitting in church gives me a chance to think about what is important in life.

IORI I've been coming to church all my life and do not want to stop. It can be a drag having to get up on Sunday mornings but once you get there it's fine. Church to me is a break. It's a chance to unwind, different from the hectic times in the rest of the week. I enjoy coming and it's relaxing.

Communion wafers are usually used to represent the bread at the Eucharist.

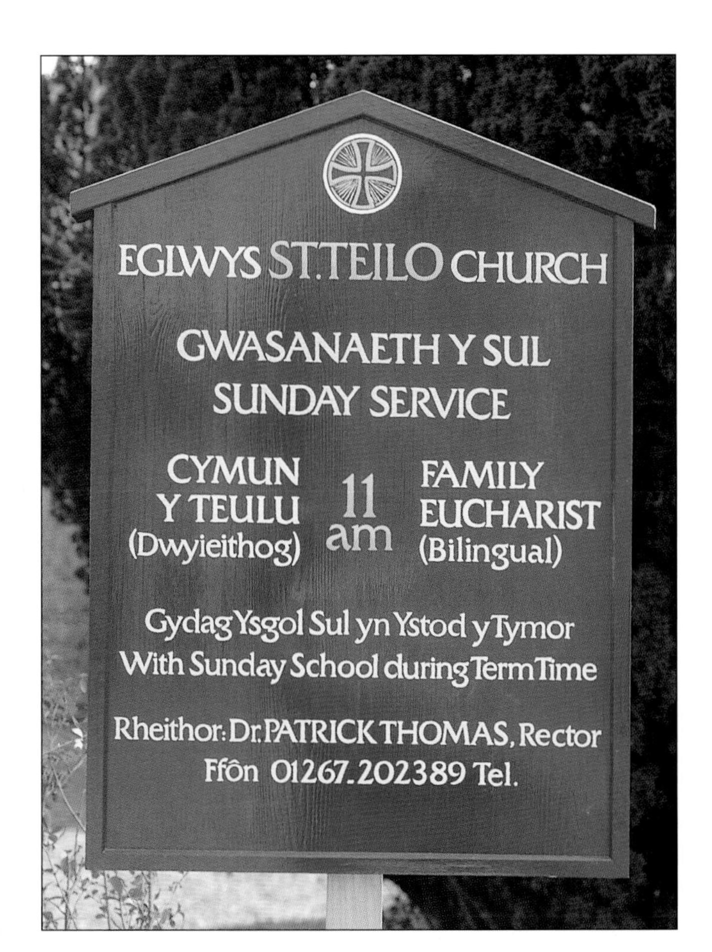

Iori: *Our Eucharist is for families, Welsh and English speakers.*

Fact file

Holy water Water that has been blessed by a priest.

Eucharist means "giving thanks". It is the part of the service when the bread and wine are taken. Eucharist is also the term given to the bread and wine when they have been blessed by the priest. In other churches this act of worship is called "Communion".

Altar A table, usually at the front of the church. It is often covered with a special cloth and has candles and a cross on it.

Things to do

The word "worship" means to show great respect for something, or someone, you value very much. What do you value in your life? Make two lists using the headings:

Things I value which money can buy
Things I value which money cannot buy

Draw three ways in which Christians worship. Next to each drawing write down what they are doing and why they are doing it. The pictures on these two pages and pages 42 to 45 will help you.

During the Mass (or Communion or Eucharist) Christians remember what Jesus said at the last supper he had with his disciples, before he was arrested and crucified. Read an account of this in the Bible, Matthew's Gospel chapter 26 verses 17 to 29. Imagine you were one of the disciples. Write an entry for your diary describing what happened at that meal. Explain how you felt when you were told that Jesus, your leader, was going to leave you.

Worshipping together 2

Ruth: *The sound of the brass band and the singing in our services makes them happy occasions. With the children it's even livelier!*

RUTH Our service on a Sunday is called a meeting. I go to worship because we always have done as a family. We praise God at our meetings. We show what we feel about God and might clap during the songs. Someone might give a testimony when they can just say what they believe in or something that's happened to them during the week that's made them stronger.

We.don't have the bread and the wine in our meetings like some churches. We believe that you can worship in all sorts of ways and don't have to do the same things every week.

We have the Lord's Prayer. We sometimes call it the Family Prayer. There are also prayers of thanks and prayers for those who need help. The captain during prayers today was asking for God's help for Nigel who is very ill. Sometimes at the end of a meeting, I might feel sad. If someone's ill and you find out about it, you feel upset because it's someone you know. Sometimes I feel happy if the meeting has gone well and I haven't been bored.

THINK ABOUT:

Do you like music? Why? Why do you think music is so important in many forms of Christian worship?

Christians pray as one way of helping them through difficult times. What things help you when things aren't going well?

Do you think Ruth and Philippa like going to church? Why do they go?

Ruth: *One of the captains will usually lead the prayers.*

Philippa: *The minister stands at the front of the chapel to lead the* ***hymn*** *singing.*

FACT FILE

Hymns Religious songs, often praising God.

PHILIPPA I don't always go to church. I go most weeks but sometimes if I'm very tired I stay home and sleep. My dad sometimes leads the worship and he asks people out to the front to help him. My favourite thing in church is Sunday School. We sing and I like singing. There are stories and we play games most weeks.

Philippa: *My dad sometimes takes the prayer meetings.*

THINGS TO DO

Look at the picture of the Salvation Army hall on the opposite page and the pictures inside Iori's and Rebecca's churches on page 40. Make a list of the main differences which you can spot.

Write a prayer for someone who is ill.

Sunday is "a day of rest" for Christians. Yet for Ruth Sunday often appears to be a very busy time. Plan out your own "day of rest", saying what you would like to do. Think about how "rest" can mean doing something different and worthwhile, instead of just being lazy!

Worshipping together 3

Sioned: In the **sermon** the minister talks about a story from the Bible.

SIONED We sing hymns in our service. I sometimes go to the Communion service. In Sunday School, we sing, have a story from the Bible, answer questions and colour pictures. Then we come back together again to pray. Every year there is a trip to Butlin's. We swim, go on the rides and really enjoy ourselves.

DAVINIA Our church feels calm and welcoming when you first go in but as the kids come it gets noisier. We use hymn books to sing from and it is really good. Our prayers come out of our heads, not out of a book. Usually people pray by themselves, but sometimes someone will be asked to pray out loud for everyone.

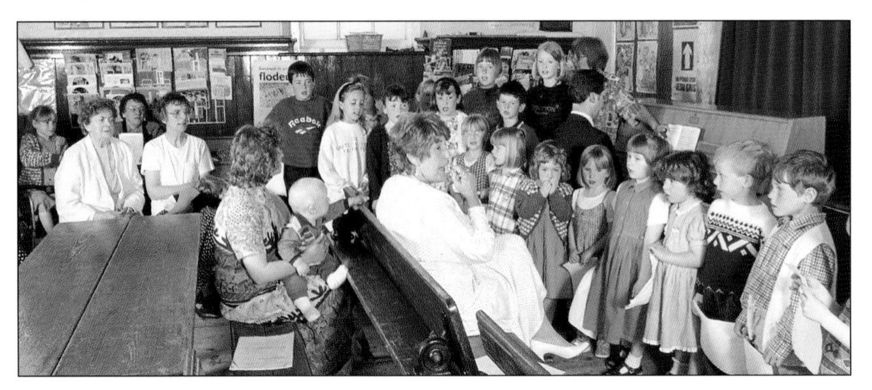

Sioned: *The service in the big chapel is a bit long for us so the children join together in another room to sing their own songs to God.*

Davinia: *The most important place in the church is the altar because that's where people go to get healing. There is a Bible on the altar and a bottle of oil for healing.*

THINK ABOUT:

The sermon in Sioned's church is often about a story from the Bible. Do you like stories? Why? Why are stories such a good way of putting across a message?

Davinia's church has a special children's church. Why do you think they might have that?

Davinia believes that going to church is fun. Why? Does this view surprise you?

Belonging to the church can be fun because you meet more people. I like going there. We have a children's church there. Sometimes we pretend to have a church service where the children act out the different things that the people in the main part of the church do. I go to church every Sunday and give an offering. An offering is money to keep the church going.

Davinia: *Worship is to show God how much we love him and it's to serve him. It's to show God we appreciate what he's done for us, like sending us Jesus.*

THINGS TO DO

Look at the different pictures of places of worship on pages 40 to 45. If you could visit one of them, which would you choose? Why? Draw the inside of the building and label as many of the parts as you can.

Look back over pages 40 to 45 and make a note of all the different objects in the churches which Christians use to help them in their worship. In groups, make a neat drawing and a label for each object you have written down. Cut them out and make a mobile from them.

Make up a list of questions to find out how many pupils in your class attend a place of worship, how often they go and why they go. Choose the best way to present your results: in writing, as a graph or chart, or perhaps on the computer.

FACT FILE

Sermon A talk given by one of the leaders of the church or chapel to help members of the congregation understand more about being a Christian.

Getting married

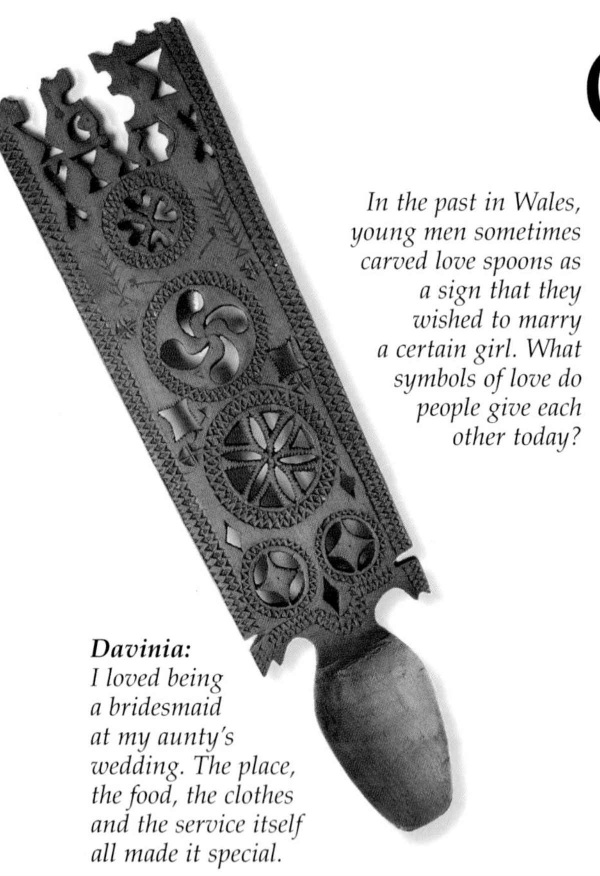

In the past in Wales, young men sometimes carved love spoons as a sign that they wished to marry a certain girl. What symbols of love do people give each other today?

DAVINIA The wedding I remember best is my Aunty Miriam's when she married my Uncle David. She got married in church. They both gave each other a ring to show their love and to show they were married. It's a sign to other people. My mum says people need God to help them love and take care of each other. Maybe that's why they get married in church. Aunty Miriam had shiny things on her dress, like diamonds, and a long train. I was a bridesmaid and she had a brilliant reception. It was at a hotel in London. My dress was white satin fabric and I had my first pair of high-heeled shoes.

Davinia: *I loved being a bridesmaid at my aunty's wedding. The place, the food, the clothes and the service itself all made it special.*

RUTH I've been to two Salvation Army weddings. Everyone was really happy. In the Army we have the same sort of service as in other churches. The captain marries them and the couple make their vows and give each other rings. Prayers are said to bless the couple and there is singing. The person who is leading the ceremony will say something about the couple and they sign the **register**. The bride wears white and the groom a suit, not his uniform. You can wear your uniform if you wish.

At the receptions I went to we had food and speeches. There was alcohol, but only for non-Army people. It was on sale for them if they chose to drink.

Sioned: *The words in the Christian wedding service mean that you are promising yourself to someone else for the rest of your life.*

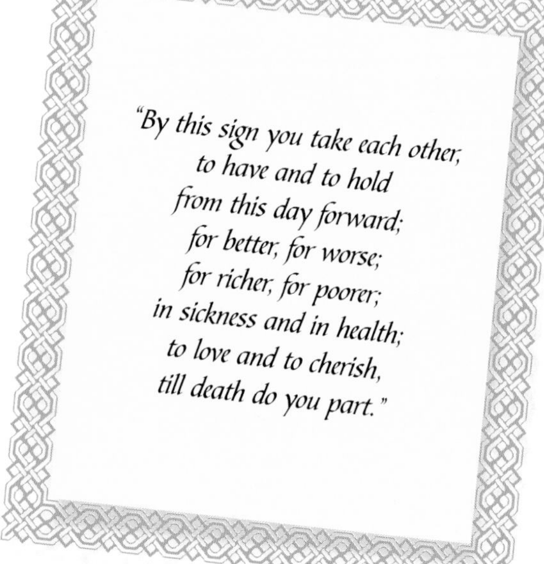

THINK ABOUT:

Have you been to a wedding? What do you remember about it?

What makes a wedding a special occasion?

Why do you think Christians choose to get married? Why do they marry in their place of worship?

Lots of wedding cards have symbols connected with marriage. Bells, lucky horseshoes, the Christian cross and Bible, are all popular.

SIONED A girl who is a Sunday School teacher was married in our chapel. Her name is Alaw. The groom's name was Gwyn. She walked down the **aisle** with her father. The minister asked the congregation if there was anything against their getting married. One thing they had to promise was to be faithful to each other.

THINGS TO DO

Make a wedding card with a suitable design on the front. You might include symbols such as rings or doves. Doves are used as a sign of a pure, fresh start to the marriage and of peace between the couple. Write a short poem or message to go inside, saying what you hope the couple will get from their marriage.

Describe a wedding you have been to or heard about. Say which part you thought was the most important and why.

Is there a special place you would choose to make an important promise? Where would it be and why would you choose it?

FACT FILE

Register The book which the newly-married couple have to sign to say they are married. Other people have to sign it to say they were witnesses to the marriage.

Aisle The open area down the middle of a church, between the pews (seats).

Being married

***Ruth:** Giving a ring is a sign of the promise made by two people to love each other for ever. Just as the ring has no end, so their love should be never-ending.*

RUTH When two people marry I suppose they're making their promises to God as well as to each other. I think a husband and wife should promise to be faithful for the rest of their lives, to look after each other.

REBECCA A marriage is not between two, it's between three people: the bride, the groom and God. For Catholics it's a holy **sacrament** just like baptism and confirmation. It could be very difficult if you marry someone who's outside the church. In a perfect world our parents would hope we would marry Catholics or other Christians. If one of a couple is not a Christian, it would be hard for them to understand how important we think marriage is.

***Rebecca:** At home there are pictures of Mam and Dad when they were younger. I think being together with the same person for such a long time is something you have to work hard at. You have to think of the other person first.*

THINK ABOUT:

What do you think Davinia means when she says that being married isn't just about being happy?

Is it always easy to show love, faithfulness and forgiveness to people you care about?

Why might it be difficult for Rebecca to marry someone who is not a Christian?

Today this man and woman have dedicated themselves to one another in unending love. They will share with one another all that life brings. Let us ask God to be with them in the years ahead.

From the Roman Catholic marriage service.

FACT FILE

Sacrament A special sign or action which brings people closer to God.

Davinia: *Getting married always makes people happy. But being married isn't just about being happy.*

THINGS TO DO

What sorts of promises do you think a couple should make at their wedding which will help them through life together? You could write them up neatly and decorate the page to make it look like an important document.

Design a symbol, or something which a husband and wife could give each other, to show that being married is something which should last for ever. Underneath write a few sentences to explain your design.

Christians say marriage gives people friendship and love and is a good way to bring up a family. Why is it good to have someone to love? What makes a good parent? Choose one of these questions and write your own answer to it.

DAVINIA Maybe I'll get married some day. I think some people get married so they'll have someone to look after them or because they want to start a family. They should love each other and not just get married because their friends are married. If you do marry you should promise to stick together and not go off with another woman or man. You shouldn't fight over who pays what bills or whatever.

Celebrating Christmas

THINK ABOUT:

Why would Rebecca have sung "Happy birthday to you" in church at Christmas?

What kinds of things do Rebecca, Davinia, Philippa and Ruth do to celebrate Christmas, at home and in their places of worship?

Why is Christmas important to Christians?

REBECCA I was amazed at school when some of the children didn't know why we were having Christmas. They thought it was just a time for having presents, something to do with Santa Claus. I think I must always have known what Christmas was really about. Mam told me that when I was two years old I started singing "Happy birthday to you" in church on Christmas morning.

DAVINIA My favourite festival is Christmas. We have special Christmas activities in church and everyone has to go up to sing a song, say a poem, do a sketch or sing in a choir. The pillars by all the seats have tinsel wrapped around them and there are balloons. We have a great big dinner, sometimes turkey or Jamaican foods like **ackie**, salt fish and **Johnny cakes**.

Davinia: *We talk about Jesus bringing light into our lives. All the Christmas lights brighten things up. It gives you the feeling that this is a special time.*

Some Christmas cards are about the Christian meaning of Christmas, some are not. Which ones are which here?

Fact File

Ackie The national fruit of Jamaica which is eaten with salt fish on special occasions.

Johnny cakes used to be called journey cakes. They are made from self-raising flour and cornmeal, mixed with water and deep fried. People would make them to take on long journeys because you can either eat them hot straightaway or keep them to eat cold.

Nativity The birth of Jesus Christ.

PHILIPPA One Christmas in church when we did the **Nativity** play I was Mary. I had to be married to this boy called Stuart and there was a real baby for Jesus. He was a fortnight old. I held him and Joseph put his arm around me. At Christmas we remember that Jesus was God's gift to the world.

RUTH My favourite festival is Christmas because of all the different services. We have Christmas parties and a New Year's Eve gathering at the hall when we all sing and see the year in together. It's good because of the feeling of togetherness. At home we have presents at Christmas and a special Christmas dinner.

Things to do

Describe the way you celebrate your favourite festival at home and, perhaps, in other places.

Candles, decorations and gifts all remind Christians of some of the important messages of Christmas. Draw your own symbol to remind people of the meaning of Christmas.

Many people who are not Christians celebrate Christmas and feel it is an important festival. Some of the reasons non-Christians have for celebrating Christmas will be the same as the reasons Christians have and some will be different. Make a list in two columns of what Christmas means for Christians and non-Christians.

Christmas is a time of joy and celebration. The decorating of churches and homes is a sign of this joy. Is there anything on this Christmas tree which might remind Christians of the Christmas story?

Celebrating Easter

***Iori:** On Palm Sunday Jesus rode into the city of Jerusalem on a donkey. He was welcomed by many in the crowd as a king, but came like a servant on a humble donkey.*

IORI On Palm Sunday we walk to the church from the top of the hill. All the children have palms to wave and we have a real donkey too. It makes the whole thing more real when you act out what happened all that time ago.

Five days later, on Good Friday, we carry a cross to a farm called Maes-y-groes. That means "the field of the cross". People used to be put to death in Maes-y-groes by a local family called the Lloyds who were a law to themselves. They used to hang people for things like trespassing in their forest. You can easily make the connection between the killing of those innocent people and Jesus' death.

The point of Easter is to remember that Jesus died for us. After he was buried it was discovered that he was no longer dead, but had come back to life.

Easter Sunday celebrates the **resurrection** of Jesus. There is a special service in our church when my father gives out pictures and models of butterflies. A caterpillar is alive, then seems to die, changing into the hard shell of a pupa, like a tomb. Then it bursts out into life again as a beautiful butterfly. It's like the Christian idea of Jesus' life being made new again after he was buried in the tomb.

THINK ABOUT:

Do you think Christmas or Easter is the more important festival for Christians? What are your reasons?

How do you think Iori feels on Good Friday as he helps to carry a cross to the hillside?

How do you think Ruth feels on Easter Sunday as she stands on the mountain and looks at the wonderful view?

***Iori:** After our march up to the field of the cross we share hot cross buns in the church hall.*

***Iori:** The cross which we carry helps us to remember what Good Friday is all about. It is re-enacting what Jesus did when he carried his cross up to **Golgotha**.*

Iori: Dad collects the butterfly symbols during the year to give out on Easter Sunday.

RUTH On Good Friday, all the churches in Cwm have a March of Witness. We go up to the top of the mountain and put the cross up. There's a meeting on Friday night. On Easter Sunday at 8 o'clock, we meet at the top of the mountain with the band and sing. We come back down and have breakfast in the Army hall. Everyone's welcome to that. I feel tired when we get up that early but it's nice and the view is lovely.

FACT FILE

Resurrection Coming back to life.

Golgotha The place where Jesus was crucified.

THINGS TO DO

Design and draw your own "resurrection" symbol.

Iori talks about the cross reminding him of both Jesus' death and the killing of people in his village long ago. At Easter, many Christians think about those who are still suffering unfairly today. Think about people who need help and make a list of them. Compare your list with a friend's. Write a prayer or poem for those people you have thought about.

Draw one picture that sums up each of the three events of Holy Week described on these pages and put them in the correct order. Colour them to fit the mood of the event, for example the Palm Sunday scene could be in brilliant, jewel-like colours fit for a king, the darkness and death of Good Friday could be in shades of grey and the Resurrection of Easter Sunday in bright, fresh colours.

When the butterfly emerges from the pupa it is like new life coming out of death.

Rebecca: *People in our church give up their own time to run charity stalls for CAFOD.*

Helping others

DAVINIA In the story of the Good Samaritan Jesus is saying it doesn't matter who you are, if you see someone who needs help you should give it. We should do unto others as we want them to do to us and help anyone in need. Our church goes to all different places to sing, to take the gospel to people and help them. We go into prisons too. Sometimes, if people are in trouble, it is important for them just to know that there is someone who cares.

REBECCA Mam supports **CAFOD**. They raise money for children in places where there is a war or a lot of poverty. Some of Anna's friends have been out to **Lourdes** to help sick people. They don't just go as pilgrims but go out to help and they have to work hard. Most are only sixteen years old and they are carrying people and putting them back in their wheel chairs. It helps you to see another side to life.

THINK ABOUT:

What are the ways in which the people in Davinia's, Philippa's and Rebecca's churches help others?

Why do Christians think it is important to help others?

If you had been saving money to give to charity, where would you send it? Where in the world are people in great need of help at the moment?

Rebecca: *Anna's friend, in the red sweatshirt, was one of those who went to help on the trip to Lourdes. They had to raise enough money to go.*

Fact file

CAFOD A Catholic charity. They sell their own products as one way of raising money to help the poor.

Lourdes A place in France which is visited by many Catholic Christians. People go on a pilgrimage to Lourdes as they believe sick people can be helped there.

TEAR Fund A Christian charity working with poor people throughout the world.

PHILIPPA We have a collection every Sunday and we use that to pay for the church buildings. Other money we collect goes to people who need our help. There are lots of different boxes in our church where we save money for charities. In our Sunday School we save for **TEAR Fund** to help people who are poor. It goes to Pakistan, Romania, Africa and other places.

Things to do

Read the story of the Good Samaritan. The Samaritan would not have been expected to help the injured person because Samaritans were often disliked. Write your own version of the story. Your good "Samaritan" might be any person you might not immediately expect to help others.

One of the reasons Christians give to charity is because Jesus tells them in the Bible to look after the poor and those in need. It can be hard for those with money to understand what it is like to be really poor. Make a list in two columns: *Luxuries* and *Necessities*. Put as many ideas as you can in each column. How many of your necessities might be luxuries to someone who is really poor?

Jesus said in Mark's Gospel, "Love your neighbour as yourself." Who is a Christian's neighbour? Does it mean the same thing as next-door neighbour? Draw four circles one inside the other. In the middle write the names of your closest family; in the second put the names of family and friends who are well known to you; in the third the people you know a little; in the fourth put people you know of but have never met. Would there be a circle big enough for all these people? How might this help you understand what Jesus meant by neighbour? Give your neighbours chart a title.

Rebecca: *Many Catholics believe that Mary, the mother of Jesus, appeared to a girl called Bernadette at Lourdes in 1858.*

Working for others

Sioned: *The weekly collection helps us to help others.*

SIONED In Sunday School we hear about trying to be the hands that help Jesus take care of people. We should try to help those who can't move a lot or people with diseases or in hospital. We go to an old people's home sometimes, singing to them and then going around with tea and biscuits.

RUTH The Salvation Army helps people in different ways. There's the soup run and helping the homeless, we do that in Cardiff. On the soup run you're out late at night, giving food, hot drinks and perhaps blankets to people who sleep out rough.

In Cwm we have a charity shop and luncheon club for anyone who wants to come. That's once a week on a Thursday. The Army people take dinners to the old people's flats down at the bottom of Cwm. I help out during the school holidays. It's hard work, but at the end of the day you feel as though you've really done something worthwhile.

Two people go up into Ebbw Vale on a Friday and Saturday night to sell the *War Cry*, that's our newspaper. We have special collections for charity, for example to help people in other countries.

THINK ABOUT:

Helping other people is a very important part of belonging to the Salvation Army. It is a way of worshipping God. What do they do to help others in Ruth's area?

What does Sioned mean when she talks about trying to be the hands that help Jesus do his work?

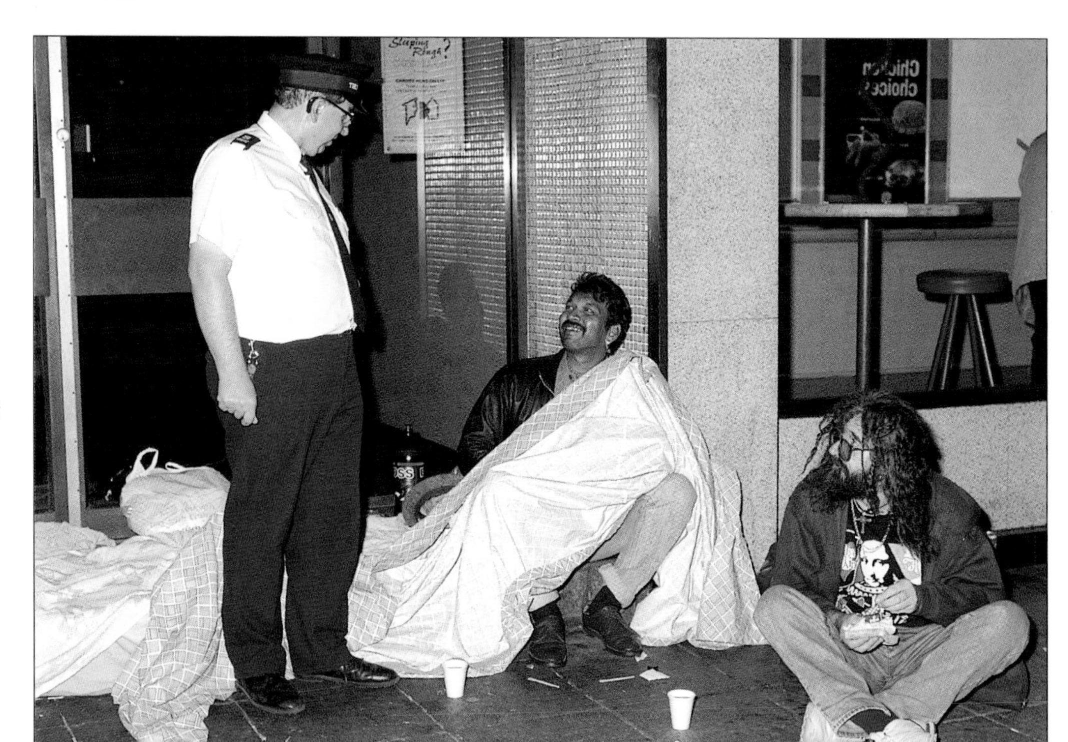

Ruth: *Doing the soup run is important but it can't be easy going out late at night. The point is that it shows the homeless that somebody cares.*

Ruth: *I sing with the band in the old people's homes in the area and read to them.*

Things to do

Make a poster asking for people to help on the Salvation Army soup run. Include a reason why it is being done.

In Sunday School, Sioned learnt about being the hands that help Jesus to do his work. Think of five ways you could be a helping hand this week. Draw around your hand and put an idea on each finger. Tick them off as you carry out your ideas.

Read the story of the lost sheep from Luke's Gospel (chapter 15, verses 1-6). Christians believe that everyone matters because every human being is part of God's family. The family is not complete if even one person feels left out and unloved. Can you think of another way of making the point that every single person is valuable and important? Use your ideas to make a poster or a "We have missed you" card for someone.

Ruth: *We get sixty to seventy people at the luncheon club because the food is really cheap. Some are old people, some are single mothers, and workmen also come along.*

Flowers are a parting gift to loved ones. Like our own lives, they do not last forever.

What happens when we die?

SIONED My grandfather died two or three years ago. He used to do all sorts of things when I was small. Then he was ill and he came to live here. When he died I felt sad thinking about how I was going to do without him. He's in heaven now. I think I'm going to see him again but I don't quite know why I think that. I was too young to go to the **funeral**.

RUTH When someone dies, they bring the coffin to the Salvation Army hall for the funeral service. Then there's a little service at the **cemetery** or at the **crematorium**. It was upsetting when someone I knew died. I didn't go to the funeral. It's up to the family whether there are flowers. If instead of flowers there's been a collection, they buy books or Bibles for the Army. Usually if someone has died, we remember them in our prayers.

THINK ABOUT:

Why is the death of someone such a sad occasion?

Why might a Christian community be drawn closer together when someone dies?

At what age do you think children should be able to attend funerals?

In some parts of the country the funeral service is often held at home. The coffin would be in the front room or outside in the ***hearse****.*

Fact file

Funeral A service held when the body is buried or cremated.

Cemetery A graveyard, where bodies are buried.

Crematorium A place where a body is burnt, instead of being buried.

Hearse A car used to carry the coffin.

IORI Eight or nine years ago a young boy in the village died from meningitis. At the funeral service prayers were said for him to carry him into his next life. My dad started collecting pictures, models and photographs of butterflies. We were too young to understand it properly at the time. In some way the butterflies were then, and still are, a way to remind us that the boy's death, any death, is not the end. I think that Christians get comfort from that belief. The children at church have been given a butterfly every Easter since he died.

Things to do

Design a card which would be suitable to send someone after a loved one has just died. What message of hope and comfort could you give?

The Easter butterflies that are given out at Iori's church began as a way of remembering someone who died. They are a sign of hope and a way of understanding that death may mean a change rather than an end. What do you think would be a good way to remember someone who has died? Draw or write about your idea.

Write about what it is like when you lose something or someone who is special to you. This can be real or imaginary.

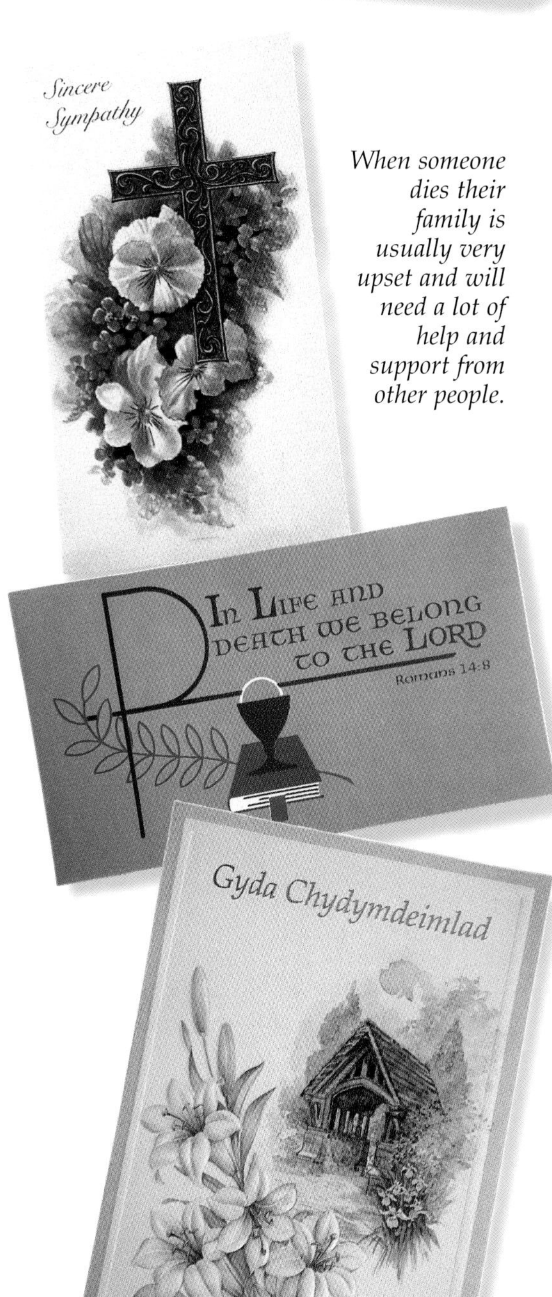

When someone dies their family is usually very upset and will need a lot of help and support from other people.

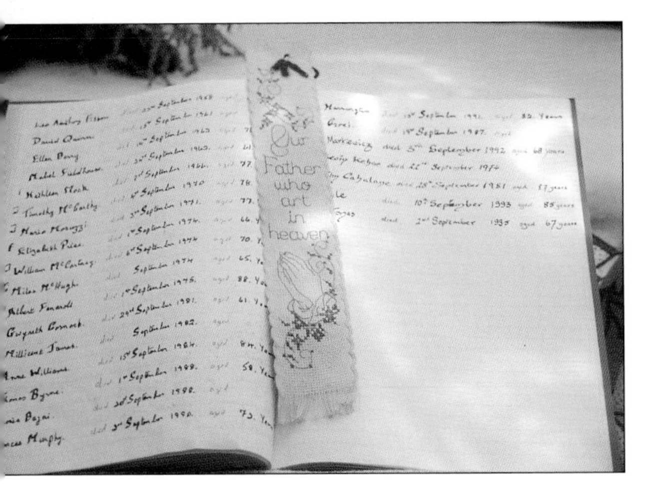

A book of remembrance, for those who have died. The bookmark has the first line of the Lord's Prayer, which talks about heaven.

What happens after we die?

RUTH I'm not sure what happens after we die. I don't believe we come back as ghosts. I don't believe in ghosts. But I think you do go to heaven to be with God. I imagine heaven as being peaceful, relaxing. Not as a physical place where your body comes back to life. It's your spirit that lives on.

REBECCA I'm not really sure what it's like in heaven. It's something to look forward to. I think it's very difficult not to go to heaven because God forgives us if we say we are sorry. I know that Jesus is going to be there.

PHILIPPA I think I'll see God in heaven but I don't know what he's like. When you die, if you're a Christian, you go to heaven. If you're not you go down to the sad place called hell. It's a sad place because you're all alone and you're not with your friends.

A gravestone can help preserve the good memories we have of our loved ones.

THINK ABOUT:

Ruth tries to describe her idea of heaven. What words would you use, if any, to describe heaven?

How do Ruth's and Rebecca's ideas about life after death differ from Philippa's and Davinia's?

Is death the end? Is there any way in which a person might live on after the death of their bodies?

Sunrise over the Sea of Galilee. Christians see death as a beginning, not as an end.

DAVINIA I knew Winsome Roach who went to church in Cardiff. She was 30 years old when she died. She was always in and out of hospital but because I knew her really well I was very upset when she died. I remember that she was quite tall and she had big eyes. She had a lovely smile. I've got some photographs of her which would help me remember her but I haven't looked at any since she died. Not yet.

Some people say if you've been bad you'll go down to the devil and there's a big fire and you'll be burnt, but I don't think there's a big fireplace where you'll be burnt. I just think nothing else happens to you. Nothing can become of you. It's the end. But if you believe in Christ there is hope.

THINGS TO DO

Draw the cycle of the sun from sunrise, to midday, to sunset, through night, to sunrise again. Underneath write a sentence or two to say why Christians see death more as a beginning than an end.

Many people use the words heaven and hell to describe places and situations they find themselves in. Write about a time that you could describe as heaven or hell.

Write about the feelings that death arouses in you. You could do this as a poem if you wish.

Index

Page numbers in ***black*** *show* Fact file *entries.*